My First Pocket Guide

Nevada

By Carole Marsh

Correlates with Nevada's SSS Social Studies Standards

The Nevada Experience™

The GALLOPADE GANG

Carole Marsh
Bob Longmeyer
Chad Beard
Cecil Anderson
Steven Saint-Laurent
Jill Sanders
Kathy Zimmer
Terry Briggs
Pat Newman
Billie Walburn
Jackie Clayton
Pam Dufresne
Cranston Davenport
Lisa Stanley
Antoinette Miller
Victoria DeJoy
Al Fortunatti
Shery Kearney

Published by GALLOPADE INTERNATIONAL

www.nevadaexperience.com

800-536-2GET • www.gallopade.com

Gallopade is proud to be a member of these educational organizations and associations:

NSSEA

ASCD

SHOPA MEMBER™
School, Home, & Office Products Association

Other Nevada Experience Products

- The Nevada Experience!
- The BIG Nevada Reproducible Activity Book
- The Nevada Coloring Book
- My First Book About Nevada!
- Nevada "Jography": A Fun Run Through Our State
- Nevada Jeopardy!: Answers and Questions About Our State
- The Nevada Experience! Sticker Pack
- The Nevada Experience! Poster/Map
- Discover Nevada CD-ROM
- Nevada "Geo" Bingo Game
- Nevada "Histo" Bingo Game

A Word From the Author... (okay, a few words)...

Hi!

Here's your own handy pocket guide about the great state of Nevada! It really will fit in a pocket—I tested it. And it really will be useful when you want to know a fact you forgot, to bone up for a test, or when your teacher says, "I wonder . . ." and you have the answer—instantly! Wow, I'm impressed!

Get smart, have fun!

Carole Marsh

Nevada Basics explores your state's symbols and their special meanings!

Nevada Geography digs up the what's where in your state!

Nevada History is like traveling through time to some of your state's great moments!

Nevada People introduces you to famous personalities and your next-door neighbors!

Nevada Places shows you where you might enjoy your next family vacation!

Nevada Nature - no preservatives here, just what Mother Nature gave to Nevada!

All the real fun stuff that we just HAD to save for its own section!

Who Named You?

Nevada's official state name is...

Nevada

State Name

Word Definition

OFFICIAL: appointed, authorized, or approved by a government or organization

Statehood: October 31, 1864

Nevada was the 36th state to join the Union.

What's In A Name?

Nevada is a Spanish word meaning "snow-clad" or "snowy." As Spanish sailors approached the California sea coast, they could see snow-capped mountains from the sea. They called them Sierra Nevada, which means "snowy range." The mountains stay snow-capped all year long. Sierra Nevada seemed like a good name for the new territory carved out of Utah in 1859, but the name was shortened to just Nevada.

State Nicknames

WHO Are You Calling Names?

Nevada is not the only name by which the state is recognized. Like many other states, Nevada has some nicknames, official or unofficial!

Sagebrush State

Silver State

Battle-born State

State Capital: Carson City

Since 1861

Established 1858

State Capital/ Capitol

Carson City was named for the famous frontiersman Christopher "Kit" Carson. It started as a trading post in 1851, and in 1858, a real settlement was laid out by prospectors from the goldfields nearby in California. In 1859, the rich Comstock Lode was discovered, and Carson City flourished. Construction of the Virginia and Truckee Railroad also contributed. Although Carson City became Nevada's capital in 1861, it was not incorporated until 1875.

Nevada's capitol was designed by Joseph Gosling in 1869. The outside of the building is made of sandstone, and the floors are made of marble. A dome at the top of the building is covered with silver!

Hannah Clapp, an educator from New York, submitted a bid to build the iron fence around the capitol and was awarded the job. It was unusual for a woman to have been awarded the contract.

Word Definition

CAPITAL: a town or city that is the official seat of government
CAPITOL: the building in which the government officials meet

State Government

Who's in Charge Here?

Nevada's GOVERNMENT has three branches

- **EXECUTIVE**
  - A governor, lieutenant governor, secretary of state, treasurer, controller, attorney general, bureau and commission members
- **LEGISLATIVE**
  - Two Houses: The Senate (21 members) House of Representatives (42 members)
- **JUDICIAL**
  - Supreme Court (1 chief justice and four associate justices) district courts, municipal courts

The number of legislators is determined by population, which is counted every 10 years; the numbers above are certain to change as Nevada grows and prospers!

State Flag

Nevada's current state flag was adopted in 1991. It features a small design of state symbols in the upper left corner on a field of cobalt blue. A silver star, representing the silver mining industry, is between two sagebrush bushes. A gold banner at the top of the star bears the words "Battle Born," and the word Nevada is in gold beneath the star. The gold on the flag represents Nevada's gold mining history.

State Seal & Motto

State Seal

The state seal of Nevada features a tunnel and miner representing the mining days, a plow and sickle for farming, a train for tourism, and a log cabin for the settlers who made Nevada into the great state it is today! A sun rising over the Sierra Nevada range in the background completes the seal. It was adopted in 1866.

Word Definition

MOTTO: a sentence, phrase, or word expressing the spirit or purpose of an organization or group

State Motto

Nevada's state motto is... All for Our Country

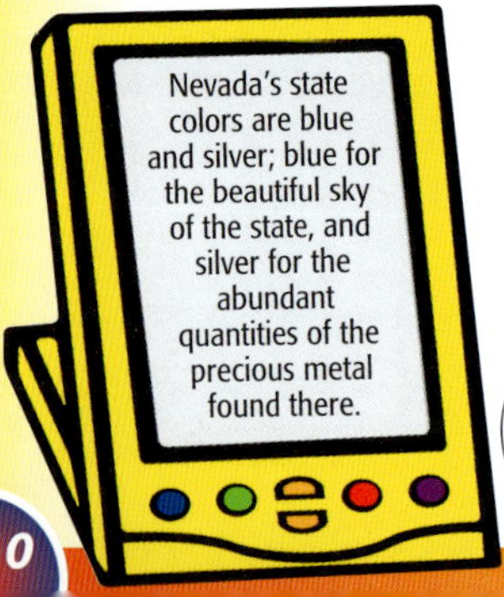

Nevada's state colors are blue and silver; blue for the beautiful sky of the state, and silver for the abundant quantities of the precious metal found there.

It was adopted on February 24, 1866. Nevada's motto shows the strong loyalty Nevadans have for the United States.

Birds of a Feather

Mountain Bluebird

Nevada's state bird is the mountain bluebird. These birds are very comfortable around people and are a common visitor at ranch houses. Mountain bluebirds usually live in pairs. The male is brighter than the female, with a sky-blue back and a lighter blue underside. The female is more gray, with some blue on her wing and tail. Mountain bluebirds mainly eat insects, which they pounce on from low tree branches. They nest in small hollows in trees, but as the number of trees decreases, bluebirds are finding it harder to find homes!

Mountain bluebirds are not known as songbirds. If they do sing, it is usually before sunrise!

Bristlecone Pine and Single-leaf Piñon

Single-leaf Piñon

In 1953, the Nevada state legislators adopted the single-leaf piñon (pronounced PIN-yuhn) as the state tree, and in 1987, they adopted the bristlecone pine as the second state tree after Ely, Nevada, schoolchildren suggested it.

Piñons are native to Nevada and produce a nut that many people like to eat. They are evergreen trees that grow on rocky slopes and hills throughout Nevada.

Bristlecone pines are one of the oldest living things in the world. Some have been found that are 4,000 years old. They grow very slowly and may take as long as 3,000 years to grow to their full height of 60 feet (18.3 meters). These pines are native to mountain areas in the United States. In Nevada they grow in Great Basin National Park.

SAGEBRUSH

To see a world in
a grain of sand.
And a heaven in
a wild flower.
—William Blake

Nevada's state flower is sagebrush. It has silvery green leaves and small white flowers. Sagebrush is actually a bush, and it's well suited for Nevada's dry, mountainous climate since it requires little water or good soil. The sagebrush provides food for Nevada's wildlife, including pronghorn, mule deer, sheep, and sage grouse.

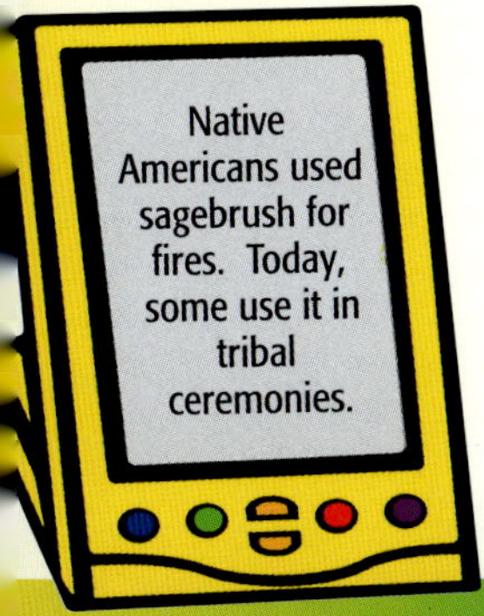

RIDDLE:
If the state flower got mixed up with the state bird, what would you have?

ANSWER: A bluebird that's able to brush its own feathers–it could happen!

DESERT BIGHORN

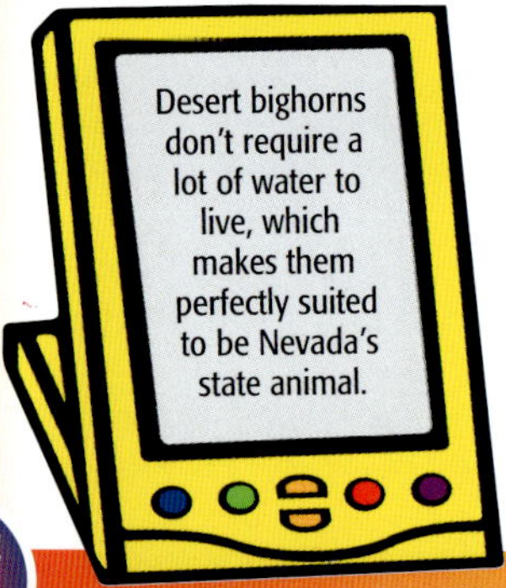

Male bighorns, or rams, can weigh up to 175 pounds (79.4 kilograms). During the mating season rams battle with each other to determine who is the strongest. Sometimes two rams will hit each other as many as 50 times, and they can crash into one another at speeds of up to 50 miles (80.5 kilometers) per hour. Sometimes the crashes are so loud they can be heard more than one mile (1.6 kilometers) away! Both male and female bighorns have horns. The female's (ewe's) horns are small spikes.

State Reptile

Desert Tortoise

Nevada's state reptile, the desert tortoise, is the largest reptile in the Southwest. It can be found in the extreme southern portions of Nevada, but they may be hard to spot. They spend most of the time hiding out in underground burrows to avoid the blazing summer heat and the frigid cold winters. They come out only in the early morning and late afternoon. Desert tortoises have a high domed shell that ranges in color from tan to black. Sometimes they have small red markings. They get most of their water from cactus fruits, but will drink water if they can find it.

Desert tortoises can reach the age of 70!

State Artifact

Tule Duck

State Artifact

Tule ducks were decoys created by early Nevadans nearly 2,000 years ago. They made them from bulrush stems, also called tule, binding the straw together in a shape resembling a canvasback duck. The decoys were placed in lakes to draw other ducks to where hunters were hiding. The hunters used darts or stones to kill the birds.

ICHTHYOSAUR

SHONISAURUS

An Ichthyosaur fossil was found in Berlin, just east of Gabbs, Nevada. These sea creatures were meat-eaters that ruled prehistoric oceans. Ichthyosaurs could grow to lengths of 60 feet (18.3 meters). They had large eyes, 12 inches (30 centimeters) in diameter. Nevada is the only state to have a complete skeleton of this fossil.

Black Fire Opal

Black fire opal was named the state gemstone. This beautiful gem is hardly ever found in North America except in the Virgin Valley of northern Nevada.

Silver

In 1977, silver was named the Nevada state metal. It is one of the most important factors in the state's economy.

Nevada's state semi-precious gemstone is Nevada turquoise, which is found in many parts of the state. The stone is also called the "jewel of the desert."

Sandstone

Much of Nevada's rugged landscape is formed of sandstone. Beautiful sandstone formations can be found in Valley of Fire State Park and Red Rock Canyon Recreational Lands near Las Vegas.

Indian Ricegrass

This tough native grass once provided food for the Nevada Indians but now provides food for the livestock and wildlife of the state. Indian ricegrass reseeds itself and grows on sites that were destroyed by fire or overgrazed.

State Fish

Lahontan Cutthroat Trout

Nevada's state fish, the Lahontan Cutthroat Trout, was named for Lake Lahontan, which covered western Nevada and northeastern California during the Ice Age. It's found in 14 of Nevada's 17 counties and has managed to survive until current times by being so hardy. It lives in cold mountain streams and lakes to the warm lowland streams and alkaline lakes where no other trout can survive. The largest Lahontan cutthroat trout came from Pyramid Lake, but those supplies have been depleted.

The state fish is the only trout native to west-central Nevada's Lahontan Basin, but its numbers have decreased sharply as humans have used it for food, more lakes have dried up, and other predator fish have been introduced into the state's waters.

Today, efforts are being made to increase the numbers of this particular trout, which have a special place in Nevada's history.

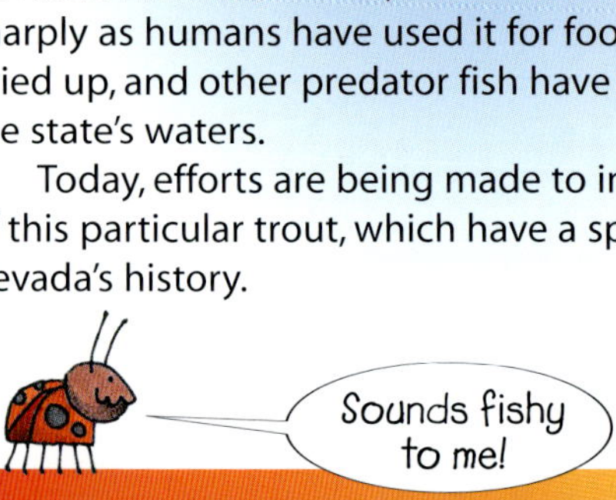

The State of Nevada

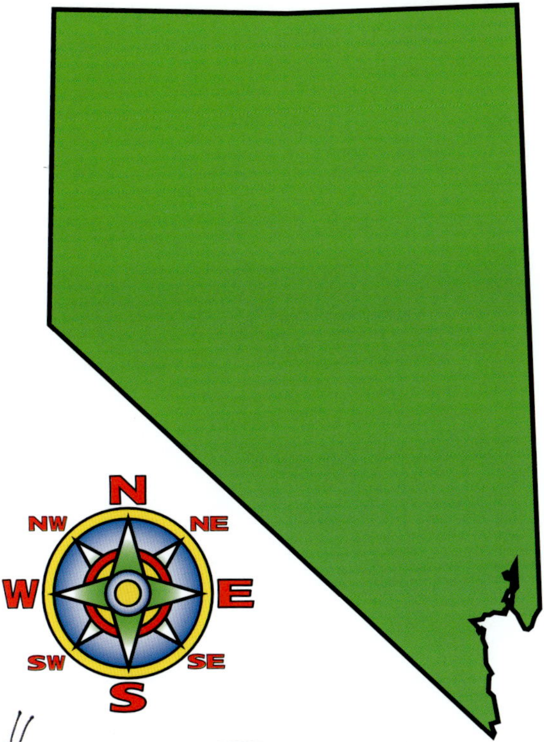

State Location

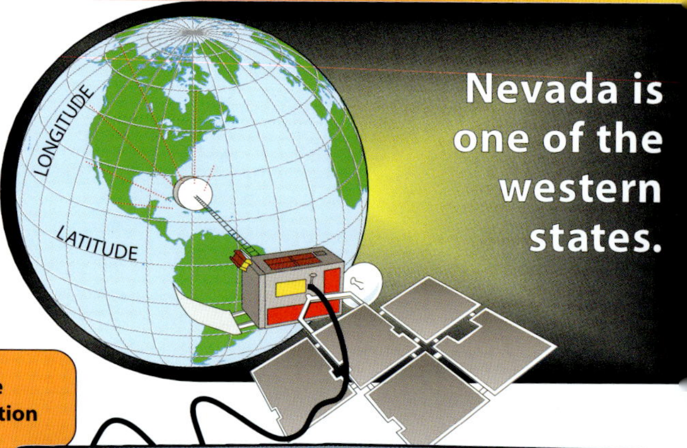

Nevada is one of the western states.

State Location

Word Definition

LATITUDE: Imaginary lines which run horizontally east and west around the globe

LONGITUDE: Imaginary lines which run vertically north and south around the globe

On The Border!

These border Nevada:

States:

California
Oregon
Idaho
Utah
Arizona

River:

The Colorado River forms the southeastern border of Nevada.

I'll Take the Low Road...

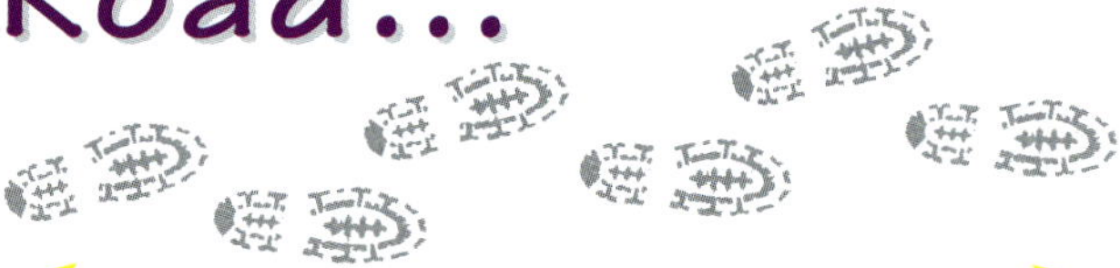

Nevada stretches 490 miles (788.6 kilometers) from north to south—or south to north. Either way, it's a long drive!

Total Area: Approximately 110,567 square miles (286,346 square kilometers)
Land Area: Approximately 109,806 square miles (284,375.6 square kilometers)

Nevada is 321 miles (516.7 kilometers) from east to west—or west to east. Either way, it's *still* a long drive!

You Take the High Road!

Highest Point

Boundary Peak—13,140 feet (4,006 meters)

Boundary Peak got its name from being so close to the Nevada-California border. In fact, it's so close that it used to be considered in California, but in 1980, new surveying techniques put it in Nevada.

Lowest Point

Colorado River—479 feet (146 meters)

I'm County-ing on You!

Nevada is divided into 17 counties.

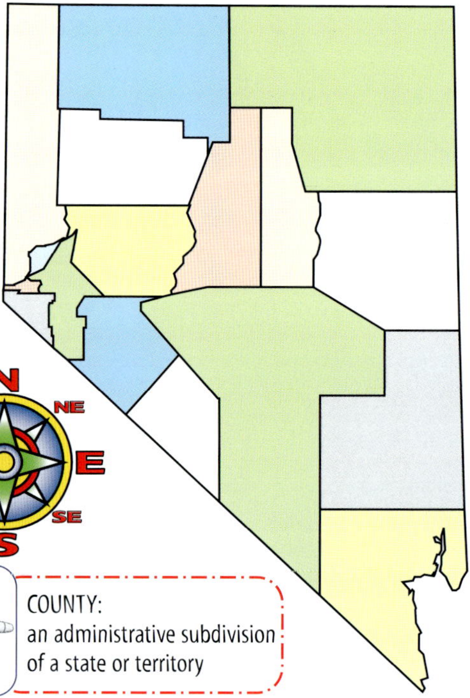

Word Definition

COUNTY:
an administrative subdivision of a state or territory

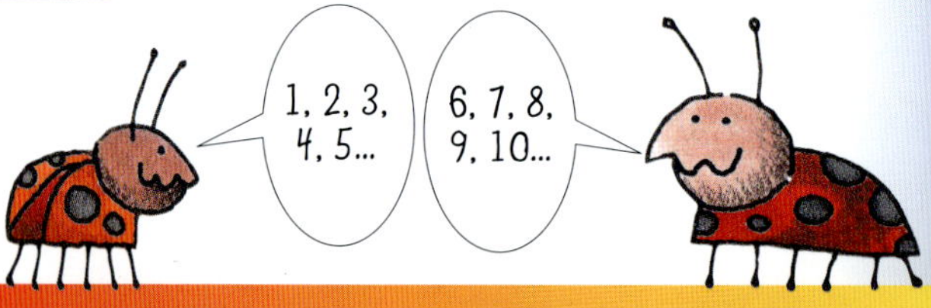

Natural Resources

It's All Natural!

Forests make up about 8,938,000 acres (3,617,208.6 hectares) in Nevada. Only 10 percent of the state is covered by timber.

Word Definition

NATURAL RESOURCES: things that exist in or are formed by nature

Minerals and rocks:

Gold
Silver
Mercury
Tungsten
Iron Ore
Lithium
Magnesite
Barite
Borates
Diatomite
Clays
Sand
Gravel
Cement
Stone
Lime
Perlite
Salt
Fluorspar

Weather, Or Not?!

Nevada's temperatures can average 43°F (6°C) in the winter and reach 90°F (32°C) in the summer.

Highest temperature: 125°F (51.6°C), Overton, June 29, 1994

°F=Degrees Fahrenheit °C=Degrees Celsius

Lowest temperature: -50°F (-46°C), San Jacinto, January 8, 1937

Nevada is the driest state in the nation. The Sierra Madre Mountains to the west keep many rain clouds from the Pacific Ocean from reaching Nevada.

BACK ON TOP

Nevada's topography includes Basin and Range, Sierra Nevadas, and Columbia Plateau.

Nevada's **BASIN AND RANGE** is part of the Great Basin, which is not a depression in the land, but actually a desert where the water drains internally rather than running off.

The **SIERRA NEVADAS** are the highest mountains in the contiguous United States.

In the **COLUMBIA PLATEAU**, streams and rivers have cut deep canyons. Lava bedrock can be found beneath the region.

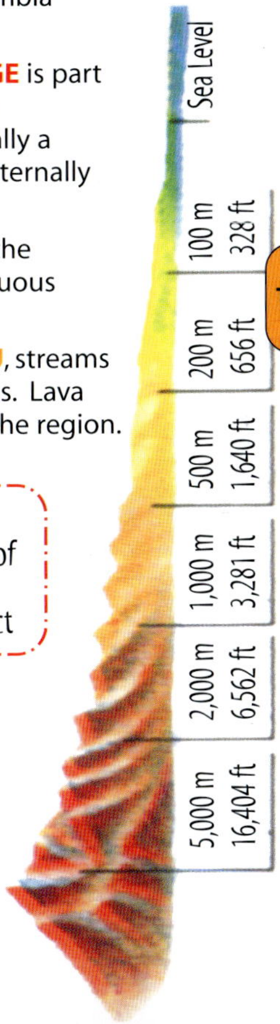

Word Definition

TOPOGRAPHY: the detailed mapping of the features of a small area or district

The Basin and Range covers almost all of Nevada, except for small areas in the southwestern and northeastern portions of Nevada.

King of the Hill

Mountains and Ranges

Humboldt Range

Santa Rosa Range

Monitor Range

Ruby Mountains

Spring Mountains

Schell Creek Range

Snake Range

Pine Forest Range

Granite Range

Excelsior Mountains

Virginia Mountains

Sahwave Mountains

Jackson Mountains

Black Rock Range

Osgood Mountains

Diamond Mountains

Butte Mountains

San Antonio Mountains

Cherry Creek Mountains

Antelope Range

Down The River

Here are some of Nevada's major rivers:

- **Humboldt River**
- **Truckee River**
- **Colorado River**
- **Carson River**
- **Walker River**
- **Virgin River**

Gone Fishin'

Major Lakes

Major lakes in Nevada include:

- LAKE TAHOE
- LAKE MEAD
- PYRAMID LAKE

Lake Tahoe is one of the deepest lakes in the world, with a depth of 1,645 feet (501 meters), but its clear water has caused it to be compared to a diamond glistening on the landscape. Objects can be seen to a depth of 75 feet (23 meters). Tahoe is a Washoe word for "big water."

Word Definition

RESERVOIR: a body of water stored for public use

ARE YOU A CITY MOUSE... OR A COUNTRY MOUSE?

Have you heard of these wonderful Nevada town, city, or crossroad names? Perhaps you can start your own list!

MAJOR CITIES:

- **Las Vegas**
- **Reno**
- **Sparks**
- **Carson City**
- **Laughlin**
- **Winnemucca**
- **Henderson**
- **Elko**
- **Denio**
- **McDermit**
- **Jarbidge**

UNIQUE NAMES:

- **Jackpot**
- **Contact**
- **Ruth**
- **Carp**
- **Dry Lake**
- **Searchlight**
- **Pahrump**
- **Gold Point**
- **Silverpeak**
- **Genoa**

Transportation

Major Interstate Highways

I-80 and I-15

Railroads

Amtrak

Union Pacific Railroad Company

Southern Pacific Transportation Company

The Transcontinental Railroad

Major Airports

Nevada has international airports in Las Vegas and Reno.

Las Vegas was the first site of a noiseless, pollution-free transportation mode called a People Mover. It whisks passengers from one point to another in cars on elevated guide rails.

Timeline

AD 1150	Anasazi mysteriously leave their civilization
1776	Spanish priest Francisco Garcés may be first European to pass through Nevada
1821	Mexico gains independence from Spain; Nevada becomes Mexican territory
1848	U.S. acquires territory including Nevada after winning Mexican-American War
1850	Mormon prospectors find gold in Gold Canyon
1851	First permanent settlement is founded by Mormons in Genoa
1864	Nevada becomes 36th state on October 31
1890	Nevada experiences population slump as demand for silver decreases
1931	Gambling legalized by state legislature
1936	Hoover Dam completed
1951	U.S. begins testing atomic weapons in Nevada
1980	State legislators pass Lake Tahoe antipollution bill
1986	Nevada's first national park, Great Basin National Park established
1990s	Laughlin becomes Nevada's third-largest gambling destination established
2001	Nevada enters the 21st century

Here come the humans!

Thousands of years ago, ancient peoples inhabited Nevada. They may have originally come across a frozen bridge of land between Asia and Alaska. If so, they slowly traveled east until some settled in what would one day become the state of Nevada.

These early people were nomadic hunters who traveled in small bands. They camped when seasons offered hunting, fishing, and fruit and nut gathering.

Native Americans Once Ruled!

As long ago as 12,000 BC, ancient peoples were settling along prehistoric lakes and rivers in Nevada. Then, about 5,000 years ago, a group known as the Lovelock Culture settled in the Humboldt Mountain Range in northern Nevada. Nearly 2,500 years later, a group called the Anasazi ("Ancient Ones") built villages in the Moapa Valley, northeast of present-day Las Vegas.

For some reason, these ancient civilizations disappeared. Experts who study ancient civilizations say disease, famine, or drought may have caused these tribes to move eastward. Some also believe that more aggressive tribes may have driven them out of their lands.

Word Definition

WAMPUM: beads, pierced and strung, used by Indians as money or for ornaments

Land Ho!

The Spanish were the first Europeans to claim the land including Nevada. This happened in 1521. However, the Spanish didn't explore the land for another 250 years. Then, in 1821, Mexico gained its independence from Spain, and Nevada was included in the Mexican territory. By the late 1820s, British trappers came into the area in search of beaver. Not until 1826 did the first American venture into the area. Then in 1848, the United States defeated Mexico in the Mexican-American War, and the United States gained the area that included Nevada.

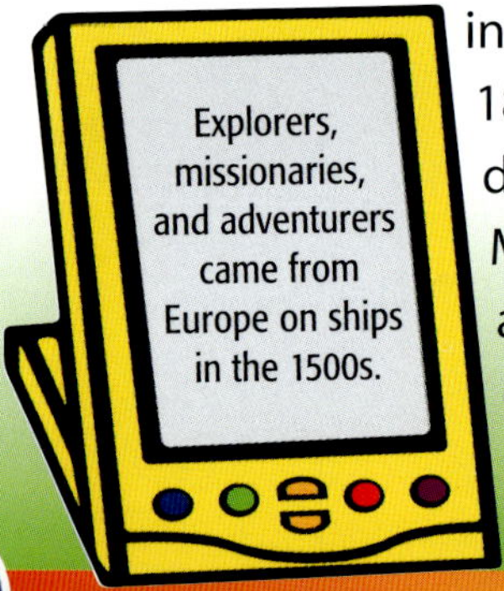

Home, Sweet Home

Life changed dramatically in the mid 1800s in Nevada after a farm foreman in California picked up a sparkly pebble from a stream. The pebble turned out to be pure gold, and the Great California Gold Rush was on! Thousands passed through the desert areas of Nevada, but most kept on moving… if they survived.

About the same time, a religious group called the Mormons had been forced to leave Illinois because of their beliefs. They eventually reached Utah and began exploring the surrounding area. In 1851, a Mormon settlement was started just south of where Reno, Nevada, is located today. No one had lived in the Nevada area since the time of the Anasazi. By the 1850s, the quest for those gold pebbles had reached Nevada and boom towns sprang up near where people were finding gold and another popular mineral, silver.

In order for a territory to become a state, the law required that 127,381 people live there. In 1861, when Nevada applied for statehood, a fraction of that many people lived there. Still, President Abraham Lincoln granted statehood on October 31, 1864.

It's Mine!

Were it not for the mining industry, settlers might not have come to Nevada in any numbers. Today, mining is the number two industry in Nevada behind tourism.

Nevada Mines

Nevada's nickname is the Silver State, and it is the nation's top producer of silver. Silver mines still in operation are most common in the southwestern part of the state. Hawthorne is the leading silver center.

Gold is still a hot commodity, too. Nevada is the top producer of gold of all the 50 states, and two-thirds of all the gold mined in the United States comes from Nevada. Only South Africa outranks Nevada in gold mining. Nevada's most productive gold mine is in Elko County, just north of Carlin.

The Nevada town of Winnemucca used to host Butch Cassidy Days each year in September. They marked the anniversary of a bank robbery pulled off by Cassidy and his gang. On September 19, 1900, Cassidy, the Sundance Kid, and the rest of the Wild Bunch, galloped into Winnemucca, and robbed the First National Bank of $32,000. They had a wild shootout before they left with their loot. Afterward, the legend says that Cassidy sent a thank-you note and a picture of himself and his boys to the bank!

However, there isn't any evidence that Butch Cassidy and the Wild Bunch ever set foot in Winnemucca—much less robbed the bank. The bank did receive a photo of Butch—from the Pinkerton Detective Agency for witnesses to see if the robbers had indeed been the Wild Bunch. Still, a $6,000 reward was offered for the arrest of the Winnemucca bank robbers with Butch Cassidy and the Sundance Kid as possible suspects. No one was ever arrested.

Freedom! Freedom!

Some settlers in the New World felt that England ignored their ideas and concerns. In 1775, the colonies went to war with England. On July 4, 1776, the Declaration of Independence was signed.

During this time, Nevada was virtually uninhabited. The Indian tribes who had settled in the area in prehistoric times, had, for the most part, abandoned their homes and fields and left.

In 1776, 250 years after the Spanish conquered Mexico, a missionary, Father Francisco Garcés, may have crossed Nevada's southern tip on his search for a new route from New Mexico to California. This would have made him the first white man to set foot in Nevada.

Slaves and Slavery

In 1859 as the United States was on the verge of entering the Civil War, silver was discovered in Nevada. People of every race flocked there, seeking fortunes. In 1860, Nevada was still a sparsely populated area. One account says that only 44 black people lived in Nevada.

Nevada Territory was created in March 1861. When the Southern states began seceding from the Union, the Nevada territory was declared a non-slave or free-soil region.

In 1865, the 13th Amendment abolished slavery in the United States. Nevada quickly ratified the 13th Amendment and the two others that guaranteed former slaves equal civil and voting rights.

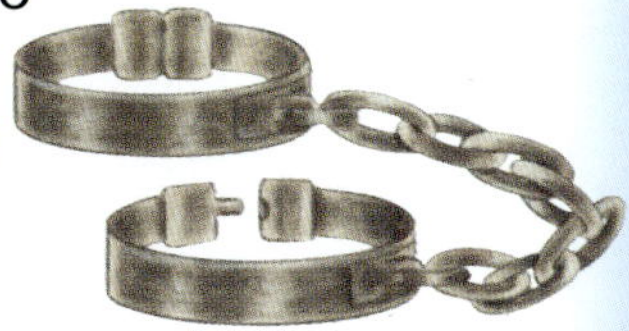

Word Definition

ABOLITIONIST: person who believed slavery was wrong and should be ended

The Civil War

Brother

The Civil War was fought between the American states. The argument was over states' rights to make their own decisions, including whether or not to own slaves. Some of the southern states began to secede (leave) the Union. They formed the Confederate States of America.

The Civil War was also called the War Between the States. Soldiers often found themselves fighting against former friends and neighbors, even brother against brother. Those who did survive often went home without an arm, leg, or both, since amputation was the "cure" for most battlefield wounds. More Americans were killed during the Civil War than during World Wars I and II together!

Word Definition

RECONSTRUCTION: the recovery and rebuilding period following the Civil War

vs. Brother

Most people living in Nevada supported the Union and opposed slavery. In fact, there were no slaves in Nevada. President Abraham Lincoln made Nevada the nation's 36th state on October 31, 1864.

President Abraham Lincoln welcomed Nevada into the Union. He would use the valuable silver being mined there to help finance the expensive Civil War.

Get It In Writing!

Famous Documents

1776
Declaration of Independence

1789
U.S. Constitution

1848
Treaty of Guadalupe Hidalgo

1858
Nevada's first newspaper,
Territorial Enterprise

1864
Nevada Constitution

Welcome to America!

People have come to Nevada from other states and many other countries on almost every continent! As time goes by, Nevada's population grows more diverse. This means that people of different races and from different cultures and ethnic backgrounds have moved to Nevada.

One group that settled in Nevada were the Basques. These people, mainly known for being sheep ranchers, began arriving more than 100 years ago. They came from the Pyrenees Mountains, which is between France and Spain. In addition to sheep ranching, the Basques also built hotels and restaurants in northern Nevada towns.

In the past, many immigrants have come to Nevada from China, Canada, Ireland, Spain, Italy, and Germany. People have migrated to Nevada from Hispanic countries such as Mexico.

Only a certain number of immigrants are allowed to move to America each year. Many of these immigrants eventually become U.S. citizens.

1846

On October 5 near Golconda, Nevada, two members of the Donner Party had an argument over a route. A party leader, James Reed, stabbed John Snyder to death. Witnesses disputed Reed's claim that he killed in self-defense. Instead of being hanged, Reed was banished. Reed's leadership skills may have helped the party later on its ill-fated trip that resulted in starvation and cannibalism. Of the original 87, only 47 survived.

1869

On April 7, a fire began at the 800-foot (244-meter) level of the Yellow Jacket Mine. Fire spread to two other mines. The Yellow Jacket Mine disaster claimed the lives of 37 miners. Three years passed before the smoldering remains of the fire were completely put out!

1875

A fire in a boarding house quickly spread among the wooden structures of Virginia City, destroying most of the town.

1980

On November 21, faulty wiring at the MGM Grand hotel in Las Vegas sparked a fire that killed 84 people. Within a year, three more victims died. Fire code violations, including lack of a sprinkler system, were discovered afterward.

Legal Stuff

1863

Nevada constitutional convention meets, but voters reject proposed constitution.

1902

Newlands Reclamation Act allows U.S. government to build dams and create irrigation projects in the West.

1909

Gambling outlawed statewide by Nevada legislators.

1918

Pittman Act requires government to agree to buy a certain amount of silver from Nevada.

1931

Legislature legalizes gambling again.

Women & Children

1865

State legislature creates first school districts

1918

Nevadan Anne Martin is first woman to run for U.S. Senate

1946

Maude Frazier is elected to Nevada legislature

1955

Nevada legislators pass a law prohibiting children from loitering in casinos

1962

At age 81, Maude Frazier is appointed lieutenant governor—the highest Nevada office ever held by a woman

1982

Barbara Vucanovich becomes Nevada's first U.S. congresswoman

Fight! Fight! Fight!

Wars which affected Nevadans:

- **Mexican-American War**
- **Civil War**
- **Spanish-American War**
- **World War I**
- **World War II**
- **Korean War**
- **Vietnam War**
- **Persian Gulf War**

The City that Never Sleeps

Las Vegas is a town that is always changing. About every 10 years or so, a landmark is torn down and replaced with an even more awesome landmark. While Las Vegas has long been known as a playground for adults, it has become more family friendly in recent years.

Claim to Fame

While children are not allowed to loiter in casinos even with adults, many hotels in Las Vegas have themes that appeal to kids as well as grownups. Someone once said you can go anywhere in the world when you go to Las Vegas. There are hotels with themes including pyramids, treasure ships, rainforests, and knights and castles. There's even a replica of a village in Venice, the Eiffel Tower in Paris, and the Statue of Liberty in New York City!

The sights of Las Vegas—all the neon, bright lights, and animated signs—are recognized everywhere!

Indian Tribes

Anasazi
Paiute

Shoshone
Washoe

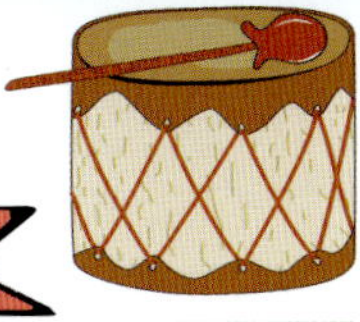

The Indians of the desert survived on a paste they made from smashed grasshoppers. They would drive colonies of the insects into a small area and smash them with flat-sided sticks!

Anasazi Indians were the first to settle in Nevada lands. This was a very civilized culture who built large houses with many rooms out of adobe. They also made brightly painted pottery and straw baskets woven so tightly they could contain water!
The Shoshone and Washoe tribes both wandered the land hunting the available game. Only the Southern Paiute tribes were known for their farming methods. A food staple for them was pine nuts.

Today, Nevada has 12 Indian reservations. The people who live on them are working to preserve their native history by holding festivals that feature traditional foods and dances, and by passing down the techniques of traditional crafts including basket weaving and cradleboard making.

The Indians of Nevada could not have known that the coming of the white man would mean an end to the way of life they had known for hundreds of years.

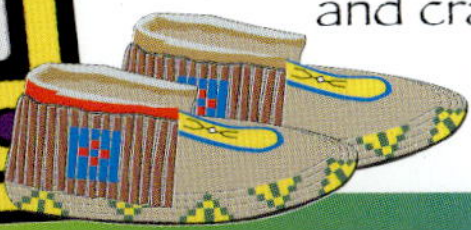

Here, There, Everywhere!

FATHER FRANCISCO GARCES—first European to see Nevada

JEDEDIAH SMITH—trapper who entered Nevada in 1826, calling it "completely barren and destitute"

PETER SKENE OGDEN—fur trapper who discovered a major river in Nevada in 1828 and named it the Humboldt

JOSEPH WALKER—mountain man who led a band of about 50 others into Nevada in 1833

JOHN C. FRÉMONT—U.S. Army officer who trekked across Nevada in 1840s, blazing trails and making maps

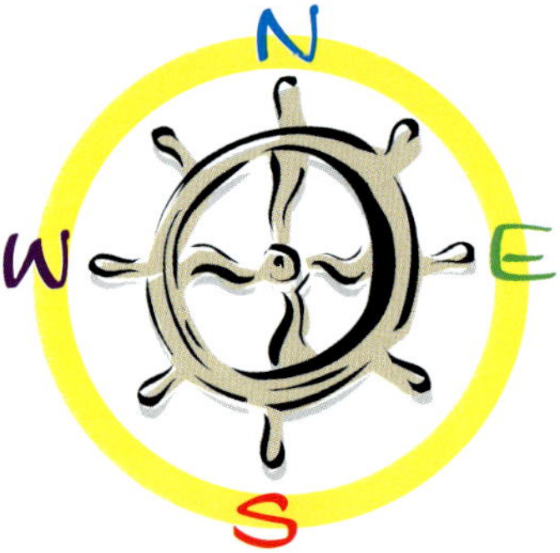

Founding Fathers

MORMONS were the first group to settle in Nevada. In 1851, they set up a fort called Mormon Station.

JAMES FINNEY was a prospector from Virginia who stumbled across the Comstock Lode, the richest deposit of silver ore ever found in the United States. He named Virginia City after his home state.

HENRY COMSTOCK was a miner most thought was insane, but the Comstock Lode was named in his honor since he seemed to be the loudest at claiming it.

Founding Mothers

SARAH ELIZABETH THOMPSON OLDS was a homesteader who settled near Twenty Mile House, between Reno and Pyramid Lake. She established a local school district.

DR. MARY FULSTONE was a female physician who came to Nevada in 1920 and delivered more than 4,000 babies.

EILLEY ORRUM BOWERS was a poor Scottish emigrant who ran a boarding house in Gold Canyon but found gold on her small claim in Gold Hill.

HANNAH CLAPP was a teacher from New York who settled in Nevada and started the first legally chartered school there. She also became the first female faculty member at the University of Nevada. A political activist, she lobbied for women to have the right to vote.

TRUCKEE—peaceful chief of the Northern Paiutes, who was nicknamed "Truckee" by white explorers; led John C. Frémont and others as they explored Nevada

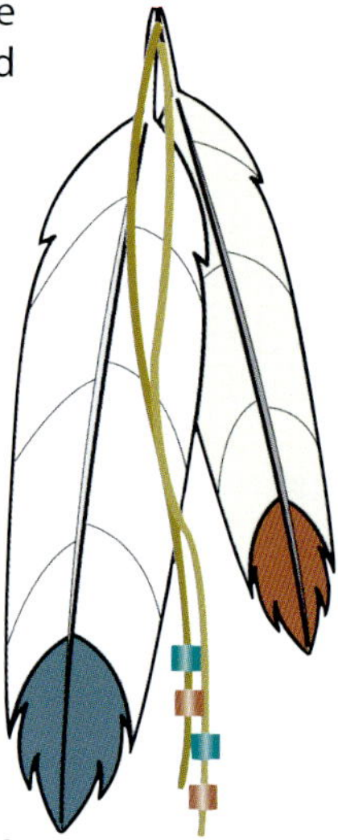

WINNEMUCCA—son of Truckee who became a Paiute chief and carried on his father's tradition of keeping peace with the settlers; signed treaty with whites to end Pyramid Lake War

WOVOKA—Yerington-born Paiute Indian prophet, also known as Jack Wilson, who established the Ghost Dance religious movement in the late 1800s

NUMAGA—Paiute chief who tried to keep his tribe from becoming involved in the Pyramid Lake War

SARAH WINNEMUCCA—daughter of chief Winnemucca who is credited with being the first Indian to write a book in English

DAT-SO-LA-LEE—member of the Washoe tribe, famous for basket weaving; Nevada legislature passed a law to preserve her work

Did Someone Say Boo!?

Virginia City is the scene of several hauntings. One location where ghosts can be found is the St. Mary's Art Center.

Originally, the center was an orphanage and hospital started by Catholic nuns known as the Daughters of Charity. Once, a fire broke out on the psychiatric ward, killing one patient and the nurse on duty. Even today, people report seeing the nurse in windows. A woman who lived in the center said she could only sleep in one bed because the ghost nurse sat on the other bed in her room. The nurse would also tuck her covers in!

Another story involves a beautiful young woman named Julia Bulette. She was murdered by a thief named John Millian. He was hanged for his crime, but Julia is said to still roam a store that was used as a mortuary when she was prepared for her funeral.

DO YOU BELIEVE IN GHOSTS?

Sports Stuff

- **ANDRE AGASSI**—tennis player from Las Vegas
- **BOB FITZSIMMONS** and **"GENTLEMAN" JIM CORBETT**—heavyweight boxers; fought in 1897 in Carson City in the first fight ever filmed
- **JACK JOHNSON** and **JAMES J. JEFFRIES**—heavyweight boxers who fought in the 1910 "Fight of the Century" in Reno
- **JERRY TARKANIAN**—basketball coach; led the University of Nevada-Las Vegas to an NCAA championship in 1990

- **JACK HILL**—Nevada Sports Hall of Famer from Tonopah; excelled in basketball, baseball, football, and track
- **JACK DEMPSEY**—prize fighter; worked as a bouncer in Wells, Nevada, bars
- **RICKY SOBERS**—professional basketball player; starred at the University of Nevada-Las Vegas

- **JACK KRAMER**—professional tennis player born in Las Vegas; was America's top tennis star in the 1940s
- **JAMES NASH**—professional baseball player; born in Hawthorne

Entertainers

★ **EMMA NEVADA**—opera singer from Austin; born Emma Wixon, but liked Nevada so well she changed her name

★ **WAYNE NEWTON**—Las Vegas and Reno performer famous for his rendition of "*Danke Schoen*"

★ **ABBY DALTON**—actress born in Las Vegas

★ **HOBART CAVANAUGH**—actor from Virginia City

★ **EDNA PURVIANCE**—actress from Reno; starred in many movies with Charlie Chaplin

★ **THE RAT PACK**—Frank Sinatra, Dean Martin, Sammy Davis Jr., Joey Bishop, and Peter Lawford; appeared regularly in Las Vegas during the 1960s and '70s

★ **LIBERACE**—pianist and entertainer; regularly appeared at the Riviera Hotel

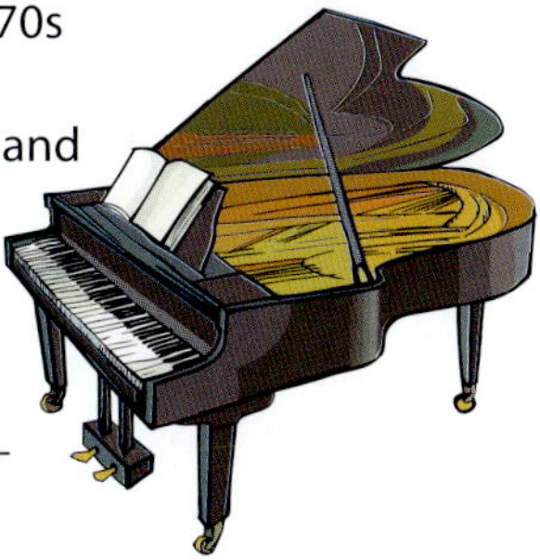

★ **BEN ALEXANDER**—actor from Garfield

Authors

SARAH WINNEMUCCA HOPKINS—Paiute chief Winnemucca's daughter who wrote *Life Among the Paiutes: Their Wrongs and Claims*

MARK TWAIN—wrote *Roughing It*, which included humorous tales of his adventures with miners, cardplayers, and other characters in the Comstock area

WALTER VAN TILLBURG CLARK—wrote *The Ox-Bow Incident*, a story about a posse that captures a group of suspected murderers and castle rustlers, but then wonders if the men are really guilty

ROBERT LAXALT—wrote *Nevada: A Bicentennial History* and *Sweet Promised Land*, a tale of his Basque father

BERTHA MUZZY (B.M.) BOWER—wrote romantic western novels often set in Nevada under the pen name of B.M. Bower because her publishers did not think readers would take a woman writer's works seriously

MARY McNAIR MATHEWS—writer who described her experiences in Virginia City in *Ten Years in Nevada; Or, Life on the Pacific Coast*

WADDIE MITCHELL—cowboy poet of Elko

NORMAN MACLEAN—writer from Reno who wrote *A River Runs Through It*

Artists

DAT-SO-LA-LEE—Washoe basketmaker whose work was known worldwide; had a basket displayed at the Carnegie Museum in Pittsburgh, Pennsylvania

LORENZO P. LATIMER—California artist; formed the Latimore Art Club in Reno, which was the only art society for many years in Nevada

ROBERT CAPLES—muralist who also did charcoal drawings of Nevada Indians

LUCILE SPIRE BRUNER—southern Nevada artist who founded the Las Vegas Art League in 1950; her works were among those collected by former first lady Nancy Reagan

BRIAN CRANE—cartoonist from Sparks who created the "Pickles" comic strip

BERTHA GRESCH—woman who didn't take up art until age 70; known as "Grandma Moses of Eldorado Canyon" for her Nevada landscapes

MARY WALKER FOSTER—Nevadan photographer

RIDDLE:

What do you get when you cross Dat-So-La-Lee's works with those of Brian Crane?

ANSWER: A basket full of laughs!

Very Important People

CHRISTOPHER "KIT" CARSON—frontiersman who guided John C. Frémont's expedition through Nevada; namesake of Carson City

BERTHA RAFFETO—Reno woman who wrote the official Nevada state song, "Home Means Nevada"

"SNOWSHOE" THOMPSON—Norwegian immigrant who quickly delivered mail in Nevada's early days by using tree bark snowshoes to whiz through snow-covered areas

ELBERT EDWARDS—historian, educator, writer from Boulder City

KATE ST. CLAIR—educator who served for 15 years as state deputy superintendent of public instruction

Very Important People

ARTHUR ST. CLAIR—husband of Kate St. Clair who was Nevada's first Rhodes Scholar to attend Oxford in England

LAURA M. ELLIS DETTENRIEDER—settler who came to Nevada in 1853 and would become Nevada's first female historian

HOWARD HUGHES—eccentric billionaire industrialist, aviator, film producer; bought a casino after being asked to vacate so other wealthy patrons could have his suite

JOHN SPARKS—rancher who introduced Hereford cattle to Nevada; town of Sparks' namesake

THELMA CATHERINE (PAT) NIXON—Ely native who was President Richard M. Nixon's wife

Major Miners

HENRY COMSTOCK—eccentric prospector who claimed ownership of southwestern Nevada's richest deposits of gold and silver, later named the Comstock Lode

JAMES FAIR—miner who discovered large quantity of gold and silver in the Consolidated Virginia Mine; organized Bank of Nevada

JOHN P. JONES—miner who made a fortune developing mineral resources in Nevada

JOHN WILLIAM MACKAY—miner who struck it rich in a section of the Comstock Lode; founded Nevada Bank of San Francisco and telegraph companies linking the U.S. to Europe

MARK REQUA—Virginia City native who was a mining engineer and built the Nevada Northern Railway; served as oil director during President Herbert Hoover's administration

FERMINIA SARRAS—woman from Nicaragua who was called the Copper Queen; she made fortunes mining, then traveled to California cities and lived extravagantly until broke; often returned to prospecting to make more money; town of Mina is named in her honor

ADOLPH SUTRO—engineer who developed the Sutro Tunnel that provided transportation, drainage, and ventilation to the Comstock mines

GEORGE WINGFIELD—financier who made a fortune from mining operations; owned 12 banks in Nevada when the stock market crashed in 1929

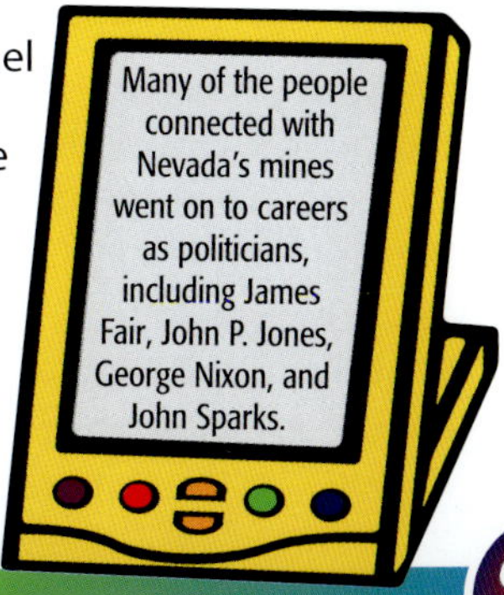

Political Leaders

EMMET D. BOYLE—Virginia City native who was Nevada's first native-born governor; elected in 1915

ORION CLEMENS—Nevada Territory's territorial secretary; brother of Samuel Clemens (Mark Twain)

PATRICK ANTHONY McCARRAN—Reno-born U.S. senator who sponsored the Internal Security Act designed to control Communists and the McCarran-Walter Act, which tightened control over aliens and immigrants

FRANCIS GRIFFITH NEWLANDS—U.S. senator and representative from Nevada; pushed the Newlands Reclamation Act of 1902, designed to ensure that money made from the sale of public lands would be used for irrigation projects

JAMES W. NYE—served as Nevada's only territorial governor and helped the territory reach statehood

KEY PITTMAN—known as the "Silver Senator" because he pushed the government to use silver in U.S. coins through his Pittman Act

CHARLES HINTON RUSSELL—Lovelock native who, while governor, worked to curb organized crime involvement in the gambling industry

WILLIAM MORRIS STEWART—authored final version of 15th Amendment, which gave black males the right to vote; pushed to make Carson City the state capital

BENJAMIN "BUGSY" SIEGEL—In 1945, Brooklyn-born mobster Bugsy Siegel headed to Las Vegas on what many thought was a crazy scheme. In the middle of the desert, he built a lavish hotel and casino, the Flamingo, which he named after his girlfriend's legs. But Bugsy didn't get to enjoy the Las Vegas rush he started; he was gunned down on June 27, 1947, at the age of 41. He hated being called "Bugsy." He got the name because he killed with such zeal that acquaintances said murdering made him "bugsy."

BUTCH CASSIDY—Butch Cassidy was born Robert Leroy Parker in Beaver, Utah, in 1866. He left his Mormon parents and took up with a cattle rustler named Mike Cassidy, whose name he adopted. Robert also worked as a butcher, hence, "Butch." Cassidy and his gang, the Wild Bunch, became notorious throughout the West for daring train and bank robberies. He and sidekick, the Sundance Kid, bought a ranch in Argentina and tried honest living but went back to robbing. Their death is a mystery. Some accounts say they were killed by South American troops in a barrage of gunfire, but others say they escaped and lived to a ripe old age.

Churches and Schools

CHURCHES
Keeping the Faith

Paradise Valley Church, Paradise Valley

Methodist Church, Austin

Saint Augustine's Catholic Church, Austin

Saint Mary's in the Mountains, Virginia City

Saint Paul's Episcopal Church, Virginia City

Presbyterian Church, Virginia City

First United Methodist Church, Carson City

Saint Peter's Episcopal Church, Carson City

Canterbury Wedding Chapel, Las Vegas

Lamoille Presbyterian Church, Lamoille

Saint Paul's Catholic Church, Winnemucca

SCHOOLS

Tuscarora School of Pottery, Tuscarora

University of Nevada, Reno

University of Nevada, Las Vegas

Mackay School of Mines, Reno

Sierra Nevada College, Incline Village

The entire state of Nevada contains fewer schools than some large cities in the East. All children between the ages of 7 and 17 are required to attend school.

VALLEY OF FIRE STATE PARK, northeast of Las Vegas—includes impressive rock formations with names such as the Beehives, Elephant Rock, and Seven Sisters

DEATH VALLEY NATIONAL PARK

LAKE MEAD NATIONAL RECREATION AREA

HUMBOLDT NATIONAL FOREST

VETERAN'S MEMORIAL PARK, Winnemucca

GREAT BASIN NATIONAL PARK, White Pine County

BERLIN-ICHTHYOSAUR STATE PARK, Berlin

Historical Homes

TOM KELLY'S BOTTLE HOUSE, Rhyolite home built with more than 20,000 discarded bottles

SCOTTY'S CASTLE, near Beatty—Mediterranean-style hacienda with a 56-foot (17-meter) high clock tower

MACKAY MANSION, Virginia City

CHOLLAR MANSION, Virginia City

BOWERS MANSION, near Carson City

MARZEN HOUSE, Lovelock

THE CASTLE, Virginia City

GOVERNOR'S MANSION, Carson City

Forts and Battle Site

A few of Nevada's famous Forts

- **FORT HALLECK**, near Wells—built to provide protection for travelers on the California Trail and workers constructing the Central Pacific Railroad

- **FORT McDERMITT**, McDermitt—site of fort built in 1865 for protection of travelers and ranchers

- **FORT CHURCHILL**, Silver Springs—constructed by U.S. Army in 1869 in wake of Pyramid Lake Indian War to protect Pony Express riders and settlers

- **OLD MORMON FORT**, Las Vegas—oldest building in Nevada

Battle Site

- **RABBIT CREEK**, north of Golconda—In February 1911, posses set out in search of a band of Shoshone and Bannock Indians who had allegedly murdered four sheep herders. The band was trapped in a canyon. Eight Indians and one posse member were killed.

Libraries

Check out the following special Nevada libraries! (Do you have a library card? Have you worn it out yet?!)

UNIVERSITY OF NEVADA, Reno—state's largest library

UNIVERSITY OF NEVADA, Las Vegas

NEVADA STATE LIBRARY, Carson City—official library for the state government

MACKAY SCHOOL OF MINES, Reno—houses a large collection of mining and minerals books

Nevada has approximately 100 public and special library systems.

Zoos and Attractions

GRIMES POINT ARCHAEOLOGICAL AREA, Fallon

STILLWATER NATIONAL WILDLIFE REFUGE, near Fallon

PAHRANAGAT NATIONAL WILDLIFE REFUGE, Pahranagat Valley

ANIMAL ARK, near Reno—nature center and wildlife refuge

CLAN ALPINE MOUNTAINS WILD STUDY AREA, Dixie Valley

FLEISCHMANN PLANETARIUM, Reno

WILBUR D. MAY ARBORETUM & BOTANICAL GARDEN, Reno

SOUTHERN NEVADA ZOOLOGICAL-BOTANICAL PARK, Las Vegas

SECRET GARDEN, Las Vegas

DESERT DEMONSTRATION GARDENS, Las Vegas

Museums

NORTHEASTERN NEVADA MUSEUM, Elko

BUCKAROO HALL OF FAME AND WESTERN HERITAGE MUSEUM, Winnemucca

NEVADA NORTHERN RAILWAY MUSEUM, Ely

GOLD WELL MUSEUM, Rhyolite

CENTRAL NEVADA MUSEUM, Tonopah

NEVADA STATE MUSEUM (CARSON CITY MINT), Carson City—includes remains of the Spirit Cave Man, the well-preserved body of an ancient man

CHILDREN'S MUSEUM, Carson City

STEWART INDIAN MUSEUM, Carson City

FOURTH WARD SCHOOL MUSEUM, Virginia City

THE WAY IT WAS MUSEUM, Virginia City

NATIONAL AUTOMOBILE MUSEUM, Reno

NATIONAL AIR RACE MUSEUM & HALL OF FAME, Sparks

LIED DISCOVERY CHILDREN'S MUSEUM, Las Vegas

GUINESS WORLD OF RECORDS MUSEUM, Las Vegas

KING TUT'S TOMB AND MUSEUM, Las Vegas

LOST CITY MUSEUM, Overton

Lest We Forget

MONUMENTS

MONUMENT TO THE LeBEAU CHILDREN, Sand Mountain—graves of three sisters, Jennie, Louise, and Emma who died within three days of each other around 1865

FORT CHURCHILL HISTORIC STATE MONUMENT, near Carson City

WARD CHARCOAL OVENS HISTORIC STATE MONUMENT, Ward—site of charcoal ovens used for mines

DEATH VALLEY NATIONAL MONUMENT, near Beatty

MORMON STATION HISTORIC STATE MONUMENT, Genoa—contains exhibits and displays from Nevada's first white settlement

***ENOLA GAY* MONUMENT**, West Wendover—the aircraft that dropped the world's first atomic bomb

MARKERS

JARBIDGE HISTORICAL MARKER, Jarbidge—site of the West's last stagecoach robbery and murder

STAR CITY HISTORIC MARKER, Ghost town where Sheba Mine was located

EUREKA OPERA HOUSE, Eureka

PLANET X, Gerlach—solar-powered pottery studio

MOAPA VALLEY ART GUILD ART GALLERY, Overton

PIPER OPERA HOUSE, Virginia City

ARTEMIS W. HAM CONCERT HALL, University of Nevada, Las Vegas

NEVADA MUSEUM OF ART, Reno

NEVADA OPERA ASSOCIATION, Reno

RENO PHILHARMONIC ORCHESTRA, Reno

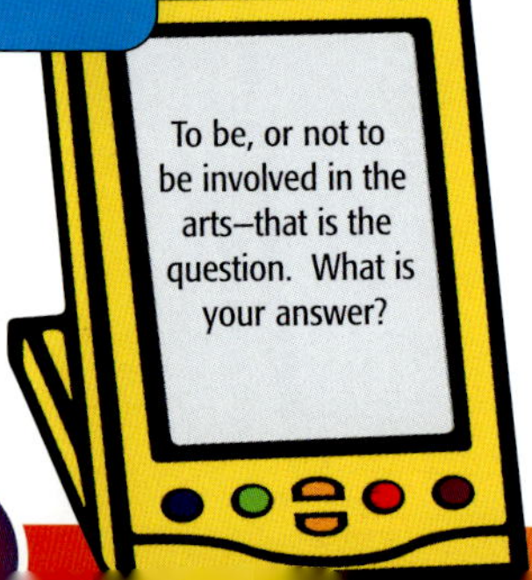

MOUNTAINS

BATTLE MOUNTAIN, Lander County—landmark whose name is a mystery as to whom was battling whom

SAND MOUNTAIN, near Fallon—600-feet (183-meter) high mountain of sand

WHEELER PEAK, Great Basin National Park—Nevada's second highest point

OVERLOOKS

COPPER MINING OVERLOOK, near Ruth

MILLER POINT OVERLOOK—Cathedral Gorge State Park

ROCK FORMATIONS

LEXINGTON ARCH, Great Basin National Park

GREAT STONE MOTHER, Pyramid Lake—rock formation on the southeast shore

RABBIT ROCK, near Laughlin

ROADS AND TRAILS

EMIGRANT TRAIL—trail that nearly 300,000 emigrants took on a trek through Nevada over a period of 30 years

EXTRATERRESTRIAL HIGHWAY, near Rachel—Route 375

HIGHWAY 50, out of Carson City—known as "Loneliest Road in America"; also traces the old Pony Express Trail

BITTER SPRINGS TRAIL, Valley of Fire—a 28-mile (45-kilometer) trail for 4-wheel drive vehicles

DAMS

HOOVER DAM, southern shore of Lake Mead—once the world's largest dam, made of 7 million tons (71 kilograms) of concrete and 300 miles (483 kilometers) of steel

DAVIS DAM, north of Laughlin—built to provide industrial, irrigational, and recreational water in Lake Mojave

MORE

VIRGINIA & TRUCKEE RAILROAD COMPANY, Virginia City

GHOST TRAIN OF OLD ELY, Ely

FIESTA QUEEN, Colorado River at Davis Dam

DESERT PRINCESS, Lake Mead

Caves, Craters, and Canyons

LEHMAN CAVES, Great Basin National Park—site contains great examples of stalactites and stalagmites

TOQUIMA CAVE, near Austin

HIDDEN CAVE, near Grimes Point… if you can find it

RED ROCK CANYON, near Las Vegas

LUNAR CRATER, between Ely and Tonopah—reminded some visitors of the moon's landscape

Question:

- Which is the stalagmite?
- Which is the stalactite?

ANSWER: Stalactites are long, tapering formations hanging from the roof of a cavern, produced by continuous watery deposits containing certain minerals. The mineral-rich water dripping from stalactites often forms conical stalagmites on the floor below.

Caves, Craters, and Canyons

Word Definition

SPELUNKER: a person who goes exploring caves for fun

SOME OF NEVADA'S ANIMALS INCLUDE:

Spiny lizard
Skink
Western toad
Burros
Mule deer
Pronghorn
Coyote

Bobcat
Mountain lion
Black bear
Scorpion
Swift fox
Mustangs

Short-horned lizard
Side-blotched lizard
Golden-mantled ground squirrel
Desert wood rat
Gila monster

When early explorers came into the region of Nevada, their horses sometimes escaped and became wild. Cowboys were sometimes able to capture and break these horses, which they prized for their stamina and strength. Today, there are nearly 30,000 wild mustangs in Nevada.

Take a Walk on the Wild Side!

Some endangered Nevada animals are:

Bonytail chub
Pahranagat roundtail chub
Virgin River chub
Cui-ui
Ash meadows speckled dace
Clover Valley speckled dace
Moapa dace
American peregrine falcon
Devils Hole pupfish
White River springfish
Razorback sucker

The Devils Hole pupfish can be found only in a pond near Death Valley Junction.

The cui-ui is a fish found only in Nevada's Pyramid Lake. Pyramid Lake was formed during the Ice Age, and while most of the surrounding area is a desert, this isolated body of water remains, but the cui-ui did not make it to any other area.

Birds

You may spy these birds in Nevada:

Wild turkey
Turkey raven
Hummingbird
Eagle
Chinese pheasant
Duck
Geese
Pelican
Partridge
Grouse
Quail
Rail
Snipe
Dove
Sage hen

A hummingbird's wings beat 75 times a second—so fast that you only see a blur! They make short squeaky sounds, but do not sing.

Don't let these Nevada bugs bug you!

Mayfly
Damselfly
Field cricket
Stick insect
Giant water bug
Water strider
Yucca moth
Spittlebug
Ground beetle
Whirligig beetle
Longhorn beetle
Ant lion
Sphinx moth

Dragonfly

Monarch butterfly

Firefly

Mosquito

Ladybug beetle

Honeybee

Insects

Fish

Swimming in Nevada's waters:

Apache trout
Humpback chub
Bonytail chub
Colorado River pikeminnow
Largemouth black bass
Rainbow trout
Channel catfish
Black crappie
Bluegill
Carp
Threadfin shad
Mosquito fish

Pond Critters

In Nevada's ponds, you may find:

- Leech
- Freshwater mussel
- Water flea
- Freshwater crayfish
- Fishing spider
- Water boatman
- Diving beetle
- Muskrat
- Hydra

Fishing spiders are also called nursery-web spiders because the female spins a web, puts her eggs inside it, and stands guard over it until the eggs hatch.

Rocks and Minerals

Rocks are solid masses of minerals or rock fragments that occur in nature. Some rocks you may find in Nevada include:

- Rhyolite
- Sandstone
- Conglomerate
- Coal
- Chert
- Flint
- Schist
- Slate
- Gneiss
- Marble
- Quartzite
- Meteorite

Minerals are the building blocks of all rocks. Most minerals are tiny and you need a magnifying glass to see them clearly. Some minerals you may find in Nevada include:

- Augite
- Iron Pyrite
- Quartz
- Calcite
- Feldspar
- Kaolinite
- Mica
- Hornblende
- Olivine

TREEMENDOUS!

These trees tower over Nevada:

JUNIPER

FIR

PINE

ALDER

ASPEN

COTTONWOOD

HEMLOCK

SPRUCE

WILLOW

JOSHUA TREE

Wildflowers

Are you crazy about these Nevada flowers?

- Cactus
- Yucca
- Sagebrush
- Squaw apple
- Cliff rose
- Mistletoe
- Larkspur
- Lupine
- Geranium
- Bluebell
- Columbine
- Queen Anne's lace
- Indian paintbrush

An Indian myth says that the Indian paintbrush flower grew from magic paintbrushes dipped in the warm, vivid colors of the setting sun.

Cream of the Crops

Agricultural products from Nevada:

Alfalfa hay

Barley

Oats

Wheat

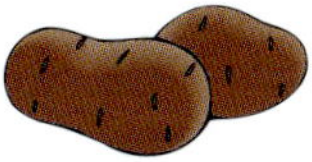
Potatoes

Onions

Cotton

Tomatoes

Hay

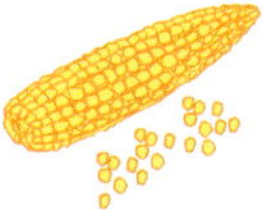
Corn

Grapes

Poultry

Cattle

Sheep

First/Big/Small/Etc.

- The Pair-O-Dice Club was the **first casino** to open on Highway 91 in 1931. This would become the Las Vegas strip.
- The **world's land speed record** was set in 1997, north of Gerlach and Empire in the Black Rock Desert. A rocket-powered car, the Thrust II was clocked at 760 miles per hour (1,223 kilometers per hour).
- Nevada has **more mountain ranges** than any other state.

- Hoover Dam is the **largest single public works project** in U.S. history.
- Las Vegas has the **most hotel rooms** of any city in the world.
- The **world's longest morse code telegram** was sent from Carson City to Washington, D.C. It was the Nevada state constitution.
- The **invention of hard hats** came about specifically for workers on Hoover Dam in 1933.
- Nevada has the only **Liberace museum**, devoted to the entertainer's life and work.
- The **world's first jeans** were invented in 1870 by Reno tailor Jacob Davis when a customer requested pants for her husband who had a 56-inch (142-centimeter) waist. Davis used material he normally used to make tents. The pants' popularity grew. Eventually, Davis sold his interest in the business to his partner—Levi Strauss.

Festivals

Celebrate!!!

Cowboy Poetry Gathering, Elko

Rhyolite Resurrection Festival, Rhyolite

Harley Days, Laughlin

Jim Butler Days, Tonopah

Las Vegas Heldorado Days, Las Vegas

Carson Valley Days, Gardnerville

Basque Festivals, Reno and Elko

Shakespeare Festival, Sand Harbor, Lake Tahoe

Spirit of Wovoka Days Powwow, Yerington

Virginia City International Camel Races, Virginia City

Snowfest at North Lake Tahoe, North Lake Tahoe

Annual Mother Earth Awakening Powwow, Carson City

Holidays

Calendar

Martin Luther King, Jr. Day, *3rd Monday in January*	Groundhog Day, *February 2*	Presidents' Day, *3rd Monday in February*
Cinco de Mayo, *May 5*	Memorial Day, *last Monday in May*	Independence Day, *July 4*
Labor Day, *1st Monday in September*	Columbus Day, *2nd Monday in October*	Veterans Day, *November 11*
		Thanksgiving, *4th Thursday in November*

Christmas, Chanukah, Kwanzaa, Vietnamese Tet, an Chinese New Year are all special celebrations in Nevad

Famous Food

Nevada is famous for...

the following foods!

Pine nuts
Beef jerky
Mormon fish chowder
Mormon split pea soup
Spaetzle
Wiener schnitzel
Mexican chilies
Onions
Posole
Corn tortillas
Enchiladas
Spanish rice
Basque shepherd's pie
Basque garlic soup

BASQUE GARLIC SOUP

Kids, get an adult to help you with this recipe!

Olive oil
6 garlic cloves, sliced
1/2 cup chopped parsley
water
3 eggs

Coat the bottom of a large skillet with oil. Heat the oil, cook the garlic until it browns. Add the parsley and enough water to cover it, filling the skillet to within 3/4 inch (2 centimeters) from the top. Bring to a boil, then reduce heat and simmer 15 minutes. Carefully drop in the eggs, one at a time. Simmer an additional 5 minutes or until the eggs are cooked.

Nevada Works!

Nevada has a diverse economy with several major industries including tourism and mining. Tourism brings in about 50 percent of the state's revenue. Las Vegas alone attracts 22 million tourists each year from all over the world.

A major employer in Nevada is the federal government. Nellis Air Force Base near Las Vegas employs thousands of civilian and military Nevadans.

Nevada is one of the least industrialized states. Because of the harsh climate, it is also not considered an agricultural leader.

Nevada Books & Websites

My First Book About Nevada by Carole Marsh
America the Beautiful: Nevada by R. Conrad Stein
Kids Learn America by Patricia Gordon and Reed C. Snow
Nevada–Fodor's Compass American Guides by Deke Castleman
Nevada Off the Beaten Path by Donna Peck
The Nevada Experience Series by Carole Marsh

Nevada Glossary

Glossary Words

ASSAYING: testing an ore to determine how much of a certain metal is in it

BOOM TOWN: community that grows very quickly, usually as the result of the discovery of a valuable resource, such as gold or silver

BONANZA: very rich deposit of ore

EVERGREEN: a tree that keeps its leaves all year long

GAMING: the term that Nevada officials prefer to use instead of gambling

HYDROELECTRICITY: electrical power produced by the force of water

LODE: the deposit of ore of some mineral that fills a crack in a rock

PETROGLYPHS: ancient rock art carved by Nevada's early residents

Nevada Spelling Bee

Here are some special Nevada-related words to learn! To take he Spelling Bee, have someone call out the words and you spell them aloud or write them on a piece of paper.

Spelling Words

atomic	miner
burro	mustang
canyon	nuclear
claim	nugget
desert	ore
glacier	pioneer
hotel	politician
irrigation	prospector
jeans	pyramid
military	telegraph

ABOUT THE AUTHOR...

CAROLE MARSH has been writing about Nevada for more than 20 years. She is the author of the popular Nevada State Stuff Series for young readers and creator along with her son, Michael Marsh, of Nevada Facts and Factivities, a CD-ROM widely used in Nevada schools. The author of more than 100 Nevada books and other supplementary educational materials on the state, Marsh is currently working on a new collection of Nevada materials for young people. Marsh correlates her Nevada materials to the Nevada learning standards. Many of her books and other materials have been inspired by or requested by Nevada teachers and librarians.

EDITORIAL ASSISTANT:

Terry Briggs

GRAPHIC DESIGNERS:

Lisa Stanley • Al Fortunatti